W9-AMP-288

DISCOVER

Sound

BY PAMELA HALL • ILLUSTRATED BY JANE YAMADA

PUBLISHED by The Child's World®
1980 Lookout Drive • Mankato, MN 56003-1705
800-599-READ • www.childsworld.com

ACKNOWLEDGMENTS
The Child's World®: Mary Berendes, Publishing Director
The Design Lab: Design
Jody Jensen Shaffer: Editing
Pamela J. Mitsakos: Photo Research

PHOTO CREDITS
© aijohn784/iStock.com: 17; franckreporter/iStock.com: cover, 1; HughStonelan/
iStock.com: 14; Ilike /Shutterstock.com: 7; joeygil/iStock.com: 13; Lokibaho/
iStock.com: 5; Monika Gniot/Shutterstock.com: 15; naluwan/Shutterstock.com:
11; paulaphoto/Shutterstock.com: 12; Ricardo Canino/Shutterstock.com: 19; rui
vale sousa/Shutterstock.com: 18; Stacey Ann Alberts/Shutterstock.com: 9 talitha_it/
Shutterstock.com: 10

ISBN 9781626873063
LCCN 2014930658

PRINTED in the United States of America • Mankato, MN
July, 2014 • PA02220

CONTENTS

CREATE VIBRATIONS

What sounds have you made today?

Did you hum or sing?

Did you whisper or shout?

Did you stomp your feet or bang a drum?

All of those sounds began the same way—
with a **vibration**. A vibration is a special way
that something moves.

Blowing air into a flute creates vibrations.

Bang a hammer and it vibrates. It moves back and forth very fast, but ever so slightly.

The hammer shakes the air around it. Vibrations move through the air in **invisible** waves.

You can't see the hammer vibrating. But you may feel the movement in your hand.

Imagine a rock tossed into a still pond. See the rings of waves in the water? Sound waves move away from the hammer the way the water ripples away from the rock.

Sound waves go on and on until they run out of energy.

Sound waves move like these ripples. However, sound travels in all directions, not just across one flat surface.

LISTEN UP

Are you close enough to the sound waves? If you are, tiny bones in your ear will vibrate.

Cupping your hand near your ear can help you hear.

Headphones let us hear things without bothering others.

The vibrations are turned into signals that go to your brain. Your brain figures out what the sound is.

What makes some sounds high? Things that make high sounds vibrate very fast. The sound waves are close together.

A violin makes high notes.

A sousaphone makes low notes.

Things that vibrate slowly make lower sounds. The sound waves are farther apart.

Why are some sounds loud? The waves are big! Softer sounds have smaller waves.

Ouch! Protect your ears when sounds are loud.

MAKE SOME NOISE

Put your hand on your throat and hum. Can you feel your **vocal cords** vibrate? The air around them vibrates, too.

Your voice is carried away on waves of sound. Now you're talking!

Vocal cords are folds of tissue inside your throat. They vibrate when you sing.

Hello, Hello, Hello, Hello. Have you ever heard your **echo**? Maybe you were in a big, empty room or a giant cave. The sound of your voice bounced off the walls and came back to you.

Yelling inside a big, open space makes an echo.

SOUND ALL AROUND

Our voices aren't the only way we use sound to **communicate**. Cell phones ring. We clap and cheer if we are excited. Sirens warn us to watch out.

Babies communicate by crying.

Dolphins make whistling and clicking sounds that travel far underwater.

Animals use sound, too. They chatter, chirp, hiss, and growl.

Low, high, loud, soft—sound is all around you. How are these sounds different?

A siren,

thunder,

a squeaky door,

and a purring cat?

Keep listening for sounds. *Swish*. Can you hear your page turning now?

LOW, HIGH, LOUD, SOFT

Low sounds have waves that are far apart.

pom-pom-po-dum

High sounds have waves that are closer together.

tweeeeet

Loud sounds have big waves.

roar

Soft sounds have smaller waves.

swish

GLOSSARY

communicate (ka-MYOO-nih-kayt): To communicate is to share information through talking, writing, or other ways. We use sound to communicate.

echo (EH-koh): An echo is a sound that bounces back to you. To hear your echo, you need lots of empty space and a big surface, such as a building or a mountain.

invisible (in-VIZ-uh-bul): Something invisible cannot be seen. Sound waves are invisible.

vibration (vy-BRAY-shun): A vibration is when something moves back and forth ever so slightly but also very quickly. Vibrations create sound waves.

vocal cords (VOH-kal KORDZ): Vocal cords are folds of tissue inside your throat. Vocal cords vibrate to help you speak.

TO LEARN MORE

In the Library

Guillain, Charlotte. *What Is Sound?*
Chicago, IL: Heinemann Library, 2009.

Pfeffer, Wendy, and Holly Keller. (illustrator).
Sounds All Around. New York: HarperCollins, 1999.

Trumbauer, Lisa. *All About Sound*. New York: Children's Press, 2004.

On the Web

Visit our Web site for lots of links about Sound:

www.childsworld.com/links

Note to Parents, Teachers, and Librarians: We routinely check our Web links to make sure they're safe, active sites—so encourage your readers to check them out!

INDEX